Endorsements

" The marriage covenant is one of the strongest covenants in the bible. In fact, the apostle Paul compares it to the relationship between Christ and the church. [Eph 6:25-32]

Drs. David and Lynn Weeter have done a masterful job of not only revealing the biblical model of a marriage, but showing, step by step how to restore a broken marriage, or one that is in danger.

I've seen them do this, and it is a testimony of the power of faith, love, and renewal.

I've seen and read many testimonies of the healing of a marriage, but none quite like what they have accomplished.

You too can see your marriage restored to a biblical standard. You can experience love and respect that is necessary and desired in every covenant relationship.

It is not easy, but it is doable. All it takes is faith, hope, love, these three; the greatest of these is love....And love never fails."

Pastor Happy Caldwell
Founder and Pastor of Agape Church
Founder and President of Victory Television Network

❝❝ In *Marriage Reborn* Doctors David and Lynn Weeter share their amazing journey from a doomed marriage to one of happiness and fulfillment. In this book you will find biblical truths and real-life solutions that will help you repair or rebuild any broken marriage if you simply apply these solutions and truths to your relationship. For decades we've seen something develop in our culture that I call "Throw Away Marriage". It's like your marriage is a Coke can. Once you've got all that you want out of it, you toss it. Unfortunately, we see that in all of Christianity as well as ministry. When the divorce rate in the church mirrors that of the culture we have a problem.

David and Lynn experienced all of the ups and downs on the marriage spectrum. They were seasoned in the scriptures, yet they found themselves at the bottom of a hole they had either dug or allowed to be dug. They didn't just "Toss the Can". They decided to go back to God's Word and listen to His instructions. They recognized the importance of their spouses' differences, and they began to see that as a strength not a negative. This set them on a journey of not just ending the divorce proceedings but rebuilding a marriage to be stronger and more fulfilling than ever before. God made each of you uniquely different. You are not a copy, and they learned to celebrate each other's strength and unique abilities.

Whether you have a good marriage or one in shambles, dig into this book and let the truths on these pages as well as the videos they make available at the end of each chapter help you either rebuild or strengthen the most precious relationship you have, Your Marriage.

Dr. Jim Willoughby
President, International Convention of Faith Ministries

❝ I've just finished David and Lynn Weeter's new book on marriage, *Marriage Reborn*, what a great book and soooo desperately needed in today's narcissistic world.

Jan and I have been married for over 60 years (to each other); so I think I write with some qualifications.

I particularly like the fact the book is very practical, down-to-earth and from real experience! I pastor a number of ministers and am shocked at the number of problems in their marriages and divorce.

My wife teaches on communication, and despite popular belief the number 1 cause of marriage failure is not sexual but an inability to communicate effectually, so chapter 3 in their book is my favorite!

Let me just add, something I learned the hard way, after the Lord, our loyalty, care and attention is to our family—not the church! When God saw Adam was lonely, He never built him a church but gave him a family! Family is Gods idea, it's the foundation of the nation."

Dr. Colin M. 'Col' Stringer
Doctor of Theology

Marriage Reborn

ISBN: 978-1-7341832-3-8

Front cover image by Brian Duffield.

First printing, 2025.

Contact@DavidWeeter.org

MARRIAGE REBORN

A Journey of
Love and Renewal

Drs. David & Lynn Weeter

Introduction

Welcome to our journey—a book designed not just to inspire but to show how the wisdom in the Bible can breathe new life into the "here and now." Let's get one thing straight from the start: this book is about real life and real faith, the kind that'll stick with you through thick and thin. See, if the Word of God doesn't work when you're out there in the messiness of life—making your way through traffic, handling those everyday bumps in the road—then, let's be honest, it's not worth much.

Here's the deal. The Bible was made for us, plain and simple. God's doing just fine; He didn't set all this up for His benefit. He set it up for our benefit, to help us through the ups and downs in real situations, even when life feels less than perfect, and especially when it feels like it is falling apart.

We all know the saying, "Thank God for the sweet by and by," but we're living in what sometimes feels like the "rotten here and now." That's where God's Word becomes practical, where it can transform your toughest days into "days of heaven on earth." The practicality of God's Word isn't just a lofty idea; it's a tool for renewal. We'll be sharing how this approach can reshape even the most challenging parts of your life because we've seen it work in ours.

This book is born from real experiences. It's not just theory. It's real-life, proven truths. We've walked this out ourselves. In fact, not too long ago, our marriage was on the rocks. We weren't just close to splitting up—Lynn actually filed for divorce. But here's the wild part. God didn't just slap a patch on it and call it a day. He took our marriage and renewed it, making it stronger, sweeter, and more passionate than it had ever been. And today, we can tell you we are better than fine. We are blessed and still improving every day!

This wasn't something we could keep to ourselves, especially when so many others may be facing similar struggles. We recently had a ministerial leader hear what we went through, and he asked us to speak about it at an international convention. He said, "I see so many ministries where things like this don't have a happy ending. But yours did, and people need to hear how." We took that to heart because, as folks who walk out the gospel, we feel it's our calling to pass along what we've learned. Our prayer is that by sharing not just what we went through but how we leaned into God's Word in practical, everyday ways, we can offer hope to those who need it most.

In this book, you'll find both Biblical foundations and practical, real-world applications. Each chapter is a step-by-step look at how God's truths play out in real life, in real-time. So pull up a chair and stay a while—you just might find a bit of "heaven on earth" right here in these words.

Notes: *Although much of this book will be phrased as if written from David's point of view i.e. "Lynn and I" this book is most definitely a joint effort in the writing.*

Also, unless otherwise denoted, the scriptures will be from the King James Version. All other versions are referenced when used.

This has been written with the thoughts of you reading it chapter by chapter, taking the time to apply what you've learned one chapter at a time before moving to the next chapter. With that understanding and for the purpose of establishing a strong foundation, we are well aware that there are certain redundancies of scripture and principles. When you see things multiple times, please take note and spend extra time establishing those things in your life and marriage.

The basis of this book was from a series we did on our podcasts. So as a bonus, you will find a QR code at the end of each chapter. Scanning the QR code with your phone's photo app will take you to a video teaching that corresponds with that chapter!

A Note from Lynn

This book has been a long time in the making. We've taken our time to shape it with care, hoping that by sharing our journey and the lessons we've learned, we can offer something meaningful to others.

One message I really want to emphasize is this: we are better when both people in a relationship are strong and able to share their perspectives. It's about creating space to truly listen to each other and being courageous enough to speak your perspective, even when it's uncomfortable. That takes boldness. That takes bravery.

Let's look at this from the example of being "equally yoked." Or, since this book is about correcting problems or potential problems, let's look at unequally yoked. Sometimes it seems that there is a hard-working horse doing all the work, while another is the slacker and not contributing their fair share. Sometimes things are not always as they seem, though. Sometimes, the one horse can be like the pushy overachiever at work who always has to one-up his coworker.

In many cases, after the coworker has repeatedly attempted to contribute to a project and been down-played by the overachiever, they simply give up. In the equestrian world, the solution to an unmatched team is for the person holding the reins (for us, that's supposed to be the Holy Spirit) to rein in the "keen" horse while encouraging the "slacker" horse. In this equestrian illustration, the casual observer might think that the overachieving horse is the leader of the team. Sometimes that might be true, but it shouldn't be. In marriage, as in horsemanship, the true leader should be the one holding the reins, and that most definitely should be the Holy Spirit.

Why does this even matter? Because an unequally yoked team is less efficient and prone to injuring both horses. The overly eager horse will experience fatigue, exhaustion, and open wounds from the uneven pressure of the yoke. The other horse may experience injuries from being dragged along, weakened spirit from just giving up, as well as open sores from the uneven pressure of the yoke.

Once the Holy Spirit has been given the opportunity to retrain the team so that they both pull together, sharing the load, something beautiful happens. They move farther, with more ease and greater efficiency. That's what we're striving for: partnership, balance, and growth together.

That's what this book is about: to empower people in their marriages to be all they can be and live their lives to the maximum of their God-given potential.

✺ *Coming Out of the Wilderness Together* ✺

Alright, let's dive right in by starting with something we think we can all agree on: the best way to get where you're going is to know where you want to end up. And the good news is, God's got a pretty clear path laid out, even when it feels like we're stumbling through a desert. Life's got its fair share of twists and turns—those seasons where you feel like you're on a dusty trail with no water in sight, just a whole lot of sunburn and sand.

So turn with us to Isaiah 43:19. Our paraphrase of this is, "The Lord says, 'Look here, I will do a new thing; now it shall spring forth. Shall you not know it? I will even make a way in the wilderness and rivers in the desert.'" That's something to hang onto right there! God's promise to bring life into our desert moments applies to so many things, whether it's marriage, parenting, or just handling the mess of everyday life. If you're feeling lost, like you're wandering around in circles, this verse is a reminder: God's got a plan, and even if it doesn't look like it, He's making a way!

When we went through some of our own wilderness seasons, that verse was like finding an oasis. The "wilderness" might sound dramatic, but anyone who's faced tough seasons in marriage knows how dry and hopeless it can feel. But there's always that promise—a river of life right in the middle of that desert if we're willing to trust God and keep walking forward.

☀ *The Peace That Fills the Gaps* ☀

Let's move over to 2 Thessalonians 3:16 for a second. It says, "Now may the Lord of Peace Himself give you peace always in every way." But here's what hit me: "peace" doesn't just mean calm and quiet. It means "nothing missing, nothing broken." Now, if you're anything like us, you've probably had times where "nothing missing" sounds about as far off as the moon. Maybe things are feeling broken, but God's promise of wholeness starts right now. Right NOW! And if He says, "I'll give you nothing missing and nothing broken," well, that's His will—whole relationships, healed hearts, and strong foundations.

Let's look at this passage in the *Amplified Translation, Classic edition.* "Now may the Lord of peace Himself grant you His peace (the peace of His kingdom) at all times and in all ways [under all circumstances and conditions, whatever comes]. The Lord [be] with you all."

At ALL times. In ALL ways. Under ALL circumstances and conditions. The Lord be with you ALL!

Not only are whole relationships, healed hearts, and strong foundations God's will, but they are His will in every single situation, and they are His will for

YOU! And they are His will for you and your marriage right NOW!

In this book, we'll walk you through the things we did wrong (oh yeah, there were plenty) so you don't have to make the same mistakes. Then, we'll share how God healed what was broken in ways we couldn't have managed on our own.

☀ *Learning to Walk in New Shoes* ☀

When Lynn and I finally quit trying to do it by our own natural mind and will and pressed more into letting God and the Holy Spirit direct our steps and change our hearts, the change came quickly. We had been reading recommended marriage books, seeking traditional counseling, listening to sermons and faith podcasts about marriage and relationships, and all the "things" like that. We were desperate, so grasping at straws can cause more problems because when they don't work, they leave you more hopeless. After all the straw grasping and missteps, though, the answer came through an inward leading and instructions to me to attend a specific church on a particular date. When I followed those instructions, the supernatural took place. But even when God does a new thing in your marriage, like giving you a fresh start, there's still that "breaking in" period—like a new pair of shoes. Those shoes fit, but they're not comfortable right away. There's a bit of rubbing and a little tightness until they start to feel like your own. And that's how it was with us, learning to walk together in this new season.

☀ *Opposites, But Made to Complement* ☀

Now, let me tell you a bit about how opposite we are. I'm a straightforward, cut-to-the-chase kind of guy. On the other hand, Lynn is all about connection and kindness, making sure everyone feels loved. She's the kind of person who wants to check on and ease people into things while I'm over here just saying, "Let's get it done."

It took us a while to realize that God put us together with these different personalities for a reason. Where I might be too quick to bulldoze, Lynn brings in a broader perspective, showing concern for the feelings of the people around us. This reminds me to slow down. Lynn's more compassionate approach helped temper my directness, while my decisiveness offered her the clarity she sometimes needed. And let me tell you, we've had to learn the hard way to appreciate each other's strengths.

☀ *Seeing Our Differences as Strengths, Not Flaws*

When we first started out, those differences felt more like obstacles than blessings. We'd see each other's opposite ways as faults rather than strengths. And I'll admit, my focus and drive sometimes turned into a one-way track, where I didn't even realize I was ignoring the people I cared about most. I could be working in the living room with the family all around me, thinking that this showed that I wanted to be with them but focused so much on my work that I did not hear the conversations taking place in my very presence. Lynn could be in the same situation but doing the exact opposite. She could be so intensely focused on trying to listen to and accommodate everyone that she stressed herself out to the point of being exhausted for days and unable to do other things that needed to be done.

This is a great time to bring up another point. It is vital to recognize that extremes can lead to misunderstandings and resentment. Ecclesiastes 7:18, particularly in the *NIV* translation, really helped us in this regard, "Do not be overrighteous, neither be overwise— why destroy yourself? Do not be overwicked, and do not be a fool—why die before your time? It is good to grasp the one and not let go of the other. Whoever fears God will avoid all extremes." This verse urges us to grasp both of our personalities as a couple without losing balance. It is commendable to have a passionate love for God, but when our innate tendencies veer into extremes—such as being overly driven or excessively accommodating—trouble can arise. As Psalm 139 reminds us, we're "fearfully and wonderfully made," each with our own strengths. God made each of us with these different pieces so we could learn to lean on each other.

But here's the deal: none of this happens without faith. You've got to believe that God really does know what He's doing and that He brought you together to learn and grow. And sometimes that means seeing your spouse's differences as assets, not annoyances.

☀ *Embracing the Process and Staying Humble* ☀

We'll go into more detail on the practical tools that helped us later, but let's just say it's a two-way street. If only one person in the marriage is willing to admit their faults and grow, it makes things a whole lot tougher. When you're both ready to look at yourselves honestly, appreciate each other's strengths, and lean on God to cover the weaknesses while growing in areas that aren't necessarily easy for our natural personalities—that's when real change happens.

So, as we go through this journey together in these chapters, remember that God's given us all unique roles, and that's exactly what makes relationships

> *You've got to believe that God really does know what He's doing and that He brought you together to learn and grow.*

so valuable. The key is seeing those differences as pieces that fit together rather than points of conflict.

Let's look at a couple of examples of how these pieces can fit together.

Lynn didn't mind utilizing my directness when it was needed. Whenever some issue or problem would come up in Lynn's "family of origin," as they call it now, her sister and she would "elect" me to deal with it because they knew that I would just meet it head-on, deal with it decisively and cut to the chase. Now, occasionally, she would have to come to me afterward and say, "You know, just a little bit of anesthesia might have been nice before the cut! You might want to give a little pain reliever now that the surgery is over!"

On the other hand, I would look to her to figure out how to minimize my intensity. Apparently, according to multiple people, my resting, "neutral" face looks anything but neutral! I definitely don't intend it to look upset or anything, but apparently, "neutral" is up to interpretation. For example, our daughter is very sensitive to people's body language, looks, etc., and she would get very upset because she thought I was giving her "the look" in a negative, angry, or disapproving way. She and Lynn talked about it, and Lynn came to me to figure out a solution. I told her I wasn't giving her "the look," but she pointed out (correctly) that it didn't matter what I intended; it mattered what our daughter perceived, so a solution was needed. After discussing with Lynn and giving her insight and input based on our daughter's personality, we came up with the solution. We gave Niki permission to point out to me anytime I wasn't paying attention and fell back into that "resting neutral" face, and I would flash some goofy-looking face with my eyes crossed and my tongue half sticking out just to reassure her that I was not mad at her.

These are the types of natural, real-life items and solutions that you have to develop!

Let's keep moving forward, trusting that God's making a way—even in the wilderness.

*To watch us on our podcast discussing **All Things New** scan the QR code below or go to:*

https://davidweeter.org/broadcast/all-things-new/

Listening to Your Spouse

🌅 *Embracing Collaboration over Compromise* 🌅

We want to tell you a little story about listening to your spouse. We've had some times that could've run a marriage right off the rails—times where, honestly, it felt like death itself was looming over us. But instead, we found out that God had a plan to pull us through right in the thick of the struggle.

Now, before we get into the nitty-gritty, let's remind you of the scriptures that laid the foundation for us. The first one is from Isaiah 43:19. It says, "Behold, I will do a new thing; now it shall spring forth; shall you not know it? I will even make a way in the wilderness and rivers in the desert." That means that even when you're knee-deep in the toughest of times, God's got a way for you. He isn't waiting for you to get out of the wilderness or desert. No, He's making a way through it right there in the mess.

Along with Isaiah 43 was 2 Thessalonians 3:16: "Now the Lord of peace himself give you peace always by all means." We want you to notice that "now." That means right now, not later, not sometime down the road, but now. It's a promise that God is right here, working things out for you even when the situation seems impossible.

☀ *Recognizing the Need for Change* ☀

This story starts in one of those seasons where life was especially tough. We had some intense stressors coming at us from all sides—personal attacks, attacks on our ministry, family issues, you name it. It got so bad that we had shifted our relationship into "business mode." You know what I'm talking about: "You do this," "I'll handle that," without any real connection. Now, don't get us wrong, we worked well together on the logistics, but we'd lost that deeper connection. We were in the same house but on totally different wavelengths.

In those years, I was traveling like crazy, sometimes over 220 nights a year in hotels. Even when I was home, my head wasn't really there. I'd be answering emails, taking calls, or planning the next trip. On the other hand, my wife was managing everything back home—our family, our kids, her own work, home-schooling. She was handling the real-life nuts and bolts stuff while I was off doing ministry. I thought I was doing my part by being out there, but what I didn't see was that she was carrying the load at home all alone.

After a number of years like this, we grew apart emotionally, mentally, spiritually, and intimately. The really bad part was that I was so focused on ministry that I was pretty much oblivious to it. Thank God Lynn was finally able to start getting it across to me that a change needed to take place, and I began seeking the Lord to find out how to accomplish that change.

The initial progress was slow and took place over the course of many years. One of the problems with this was that I didn't talk to Lynn about this process. From her perspective, there wasn't any change, and she had no indication from any communication between us to help clue her in that I was even trying to change. The disagreement that finally led to the decision to go to counseling included me telling her that I had talked to some close friends and I was in the right and she just wasn't understanding. So, from her perspective, even once I agreed to counsel with the Christian Word of Faith couple I decided to go with, she felt that she was going into a stacked court where she would be told she was the only one in the wrong.

She didn't know that during the previous several years, the Lord started working on me, chipping away bit by bit, making tiny changes in my heart. One day, He told me to go to a specific church service. Now, I'd never been to this church or even met the pastor, but I just knew I was supposed to be there. So, I went, and the pastor read Jeremiah 7. He went off into his message, but the Holy Spirit stopped me right there in that scripture, and I heard God speak directly to my heart.

Jeremiah 7:13, 23-26 in the *Amplified Classic Version* says, "And now, because you have done all these things, says the Lord, and [because] when I spoke to you persistently [even rising up early and speaking], you did not listen, and when I called you, you did not answer, But this thing I did command them: Listen to and obey My voice, and I will be your God and you will be My people; and walk in the whole way that I command you, that it may be well with you. But they would not listen to and obey Me or bend their ear [to Me], but followed the counsels and the stubborn promptings of their own evil hearts and minds, and they turned their backs and went in reverse instead of forward. Since the day that your fathers came forth out of the land of Egypt to this day, I have persistently sent to you all My servants, the prophets, sending them daily, early and late. Yet the people would not listen to and obey Me or bend their ears [to Me], but stiffened their necks and behaved worse than their fathers."

Then the Holy Spirit read it to me Himself, and here is His translation directly to me. "I spoke and spoke and spoke to you through Lynn. I sent her as a messenger, but you didn't pay attention and you went backward and not forward. You didn't pay attention, and you stiffened your neck, and you are doing worse than your father. Now, that hit hard. I realized that my wife had been speaking to me for years, trying to share her heart and insight from the Lord, but I'd tuned her out. I was so wrapped up in my own perspective that I wasn't even listening to her.

✺ *Relearning to Listen and Value Each Other* ✺

The truth was, I was so focused on my work and my view of "ministry" that I couldn't see what was happening right in front of me. Lynn had insights and guidance for our family, things she'd been trying to tell me, but I brushed her off, thinking I had all the answers. I treated her words as less important, convinced that my "graduate level" knowledge was the only way to go when, really, she was getting her own education from God's Word—an education on how to apply faith at home, with our kids, and in everyday life.

Let us show you an example of how satan was able to use all of this together to his advantage. I would call and ask Lynn if she had watched the service I was a part of the night before, trying to see if she was even interested in ministry and spiritual things, if she was involved and studying in depth in these things, or if she just wanted to do her daily stuff with the children. She would explain that she hadn't because of a ball game that our son had or some other thing that was happening at the time. Did I follow up and ask if she watched it later when she wasn't busy? Nope. Did she watch them later when she was able? Yep. Now, here's the other side. She didn't volunteer the information that she had watched them later, either! Part of the reason she didn't volunteer that information was that sometimes, when she would share about a message she had listened to and what she had gotten out of the message, I would often view what she had gotten out of it as an insignificant insight and that she was missing the main point that was trying to be taught. That view further reinforced my opinion that she was just simply spiritually immature and not really interested in spiritual things anyway!

... marraige isn't about one person being "right."

I remember one time when she told me about a lesson she'd heard, and I thought, "She doesn't get it the way I do." But what I didn't realize was that she was seeing things from a different angle, one that was just as valuable. It's like climbing a mountain. When you're on one side, you might see trees and streams. But from the other side, there's a whole new landscape— clearings, caves, and views you couldn't see before. I was so focused on my side of the mountain that I couldn't see her side.

☀ *Working Together in Faith* ☀

I had to realize that marriage isn't about one person being "right." It's about bringing both perspectives together to create something better. Genesis 2:18 tells us,

"It is not good that man should be alone; I will make him a help meet for him." Now, a lot of guys think "help meet" means their wife is just there to back them up, but that's not what the Bible's saying. In Hebrew, the word "ezer" (help) actually means the kind of help that God provides—help that surrounds you, strengthens you, and lifts you up.

When we think of our wives as our God-given partners, not just assistants, we see the blessing that God intended. It's not a matter of her being the "Holy Ghost" for me, but rather that God speaks through her just as He speaks through me. It's no coincidence that it's the very same Hebrew word used to describe the help that a wife is supposed to provide to her husband as it is to describe the help that God Himself provides to us! I had to let go of my ego and start paying attention to what God was trying to show me through her. The first step in that process, as with most things, was to make a decision to obey the Word. It really sunk into my spirit at that service, but quite honestly, it is a continual process of mind renewal (and I've given Lynn "permission" to draw my attention to the times when I need to press into a little more mind renewal. Always keep in mind that if your wife is married to you in actual covenant, then she has access to all of the anointings, the gifting, the graces, and everything that you need, husbands, to bring you up to the level you cannot get to on your own!

And the more we worked through this, the more we understood that it wasn't about compromise— it was about collaboration. When you compromise, you're both giving up something, and no one's truly happy. However, in collaboration, you combine strengths to create something even better than you could have made alone. That's what God was calling us to do: bring our different perspectives together to build something that could multiply, not just add up.

As men, it's easy to think, "I'd die for my wife." But love isn't just about making grand gestures; it's about being there every day, listening, and valuing her perspective. It's not just listening, but COMMUNICATING! As you'll see in the next chapter, there is a big difference. If you want your marriage to thrive, you have to be a "doer of the Word," as James 1:22 says. Don't just read or hear it; live it out. And when both partners are living in God's love, everything else falls into place.

To watch us speaking about this topic on our broadcast, scan the QR code below or type in:

https://davidweeter.org/broadcast/ listening-to-your-spouse/

CHAPTER

3

Communicate

☀ *Speaking Life into Your Marriage* ☀

Let's dive into the subject of communication—the backbone of a healthy marriage. We're talking about keeping your words honest, loving, and fit for the moment (Ephesians 4:29 *ESV* and Proverbs 15:23 *KJV*), especially when life gets busy. It's about being real with each other and keeping that bond strong, whether you're hashing out car schedules or dealing with life's more significant challenges.

Let's review our foundational scriptures: Isaiah 43:19. This time from the *Amplified Classic Version,* and it reads:

"Behold, I am doing a new thing; now it springs forth. Do you not perceive and know it, and will you not give heed to it? I will even make a way in the wilderness and rivers in the desert."

There's no marriage that's so dry God can't bring life to it. Whether you're in a season of love or a tough patch, He can make a way in the wilderness. There is no relationship that is beyond repair, no connection beyond the reach of God's refreshment. If there's a weedy wilderness or dry riverbed in your marriage, rest assured that God can renew and restore it!

In our daily lives, peace might seem hard to find, but remember, in 2 Thessalonians 3:16, we are promised: "Now may the Lord of peace Himself give you peace always in every way." God's peace is present in all situations, but it requires us to stand firm, to walk it out in faith one step at a time, and to lean on Him—even when our own words and emotions threaten to create strife. Peace isn't just the absence of conflict; it's wholeness, completeness, and unity in every area. For our relationships to thrive, we need to cultivate this peace actively.

☀ *Communication: Speak Life or Nothing At All* ☀

Now, let's get to communication, starting with Ephesians 4:29. This verse is another one from the *Amplified Classic Version*:

"Let no foul or polluting language, nor evil word, nor unwholesome or worthless talk [ever] come out of your mouth, but only such [speech] as is good and beneficial to the spiritual progress of others, as is fitting to the need and the occasion, that it may be a blessing and give grace (God's favor) to those who hear it."

Some folks might say, "Well, I don't curse or talk down to my spouse." And that's a great start. But that word 'ever'—that's a big one. "Ever" means not even in rush-hour traffic or when the kids are acting up. And it doesn't just mean avoiding foul language; it's about keeping words pure and beneficial. And remember this: communicating well often requires patience and grace, especially when emotions run high or we're discussing tricky topics.

God tells us to use words that are good for the "spiritual progress of others." So, before we speak, we've got to ask, "Is this going to help my spouse's growth, or is it just going to stir up strife?" Intentional, God-centered communication can transform any relationship, even in the wilderness of miscommunication or the desert of silence.

☀ *Keeping it Real in Your Home* ☀

Here's where folks sometimes get "churchy." They think about this verse as if it only applies at church or when talking to folks outside the home. But what about when you're talking about regular life stuff? Like, who's taking the car for an oil change, or who's doing school pickup?

Real communication is not just for church—it's for the kitchen, the living room, the bedroom, and the minivan. Communication means being genuine about ALL of life. This means talking about what matters, whether it's coordinating schedules or talking about the intimate parts of marriage. Nothing is too small or too personal to talk about with the right heart.

And when it comes to words, be mindful of the little foxes—those sneaky thoughts of bitterness or frustration that lead to angry outbursts. Words of hate or division can tear down what you're building together, so keep a watch on those.

Speaking of these little foxes, this is a great place to point out another aspect of the words you speak. Always remember that we are constantly dealing with two different kingdoms, or systems, while we live on this earth. Our kingdom of God is where Jesus is Lord, and the kingdom of the world is where satan is the god of this world. Both systems have angelic beings. Our kingdom has the angels of the Lord that have been sent forth to act on our behalf (Hebrews 1:14), and the world's system has the fallen angels who answer to satan.

Now, let's look at an extremely important principle that is vital to understand. Psalm 103:20, "Bless the Lord, ye his angels, that excel in strength, that do his commandments, hearkening unto the voice of his word." We usually think of this (and rightly so) in light of our Lord, Jesus, and His angels; however, the same principle applies to the "lord" of this world and his angels. But notice one other thing: this Scripture does not say that they hearken (hear and obey) their lord's word. It says that they hear and obey the VOICE of his word!

This is why it is crucial to be speaking, giving voice to, the Word of our Lord into our marriages! Words of love, compassion, kindness. Words that line up with Ephesians chapter four.

When you give voice to the words of satan, words that are of the kingdom of darkness, words of anger, hate, destruction, then those little foxes, those little devils, hear and obey those words and can cause all kinds of destruction in our marriages.

☀ *Learning to Navigate Disagreements* ☀

Life's going to throw times at y'all where you both need something at the same time, and it just doesn't seem to add up. For example, you both need the car at 2 o'clock. It's so easy just to let that turn into an argument: "Well, *I* need it!" "Well, *I* need it more!"

> *This is why it is crucial to be speaking, giving voice to, the Word of our Lord into our marriages!*

Yes, you must keep strife out at all costs because of James 3:16, "For where envying and STRIFE is, there is confusion and EVERY evil work." But disagreements don't have to mean strife. There's a way to navigate these things. Sometimes, just coming to the table with a heart ready to collaborate instead of arguing changes the whole tone. Try, "How can we work this out?" instead of digging in your heels. And remember, this is the person you committed to—your covenant partner! If push comes to shove, you'd give them the car and find a way to make do because that's what partnership is all about.

☀ God's Voice in Your Spouse ☀

For years, I thought, "Hey, I'm out here spending all this time in the Word and learning. If she says something different, it can't be right." Boy, was I wrong! God got my attention on this one. He said, "I'm speaking through her, and you're not listening."

Whether it's the husband or the wife that's speaking up, we each need to listen. God has a way of working through the person right next to us, so if we're too busy to hear our spouse, we might just miss what He's trying to say.

☀ Speaking Up: Following Esther's Example ☀

One powerful example that God gave Lynn was the story of Esther. Esther was called to speak to the king—a decision that carried enormous risk because, in her time, approaching the king without being summoned could mean death. Yet, despite her fear, she knew she had a responsibility to speak up for what was right. She trusted God's timing and His prompting, even when the consequences seemed daunting.

In much the same way, there were countless times when Lynn felt the need to talk to me about something important. Yet, she was often advised by well-meaning people, *"Just take it to God and let Him deal with it."*

But what they didn't realize was that God was, in fact, trying to speak—through her.

We had already discussed in Chapter 2 how a wife is called to be a helper in the way that God Himself helps. That meant that sometimes, Lynn was the vessel through which God was communicating. There were moments when God urged her to bring something to my attention, but she hesitated—whether from exhaustion, busyness, or fear of how I might react. In those moments of hesitation, she was unintentionally being disobedient to what God was asking her to do.

Eventually, though, she would press through and speak up. She would say, *"We really need to take some time to talk about this,"* or, *"I think we're on the wrong track here."* She learned to follow Esther's example, setting aside the fear of my reaction and trusting that God had a reason for prompting her to speak.

Now, to be fair, at that time, she did have legitimate concerns about how I might respond. I had never done anything to make her fear for her or the children's physical safety, but the anger simmering under the surface put the whole house in a state of unrest and walking on eggshells. There were even still moments—especially in the early days after the miracle weekend —when I would tense up during our conversations. The old habits of communication don't disappear overnight. But even then, she could see past my initial reactions and trust that I would work through them. She had faith that God was at work, not only in what He was asking her to say but also in how He was shaping me to receive it.

The lesson in all of this is simple yet profound: When God prompts you to speak, don't let fear, fatigue, or hesitation hold you back. When He places something on your heart, trust that He has a reason for it. Like Esther, step forward in faith. Speak when He tells you to speak. Trust that He is in control of the outcome.

☀ *Stay Tender-Hearted and Listen* ☀

A big part of getting this right is being tender-hearted toward each other. And sometimes, that's not as easy as it sounds. Deuteronomy 10:16 tells us about circumcising the heart—keeping it tender. For us guys, even hearing the word circumcision makes us wince, but here, it means being tender-hearted.

We've all got "our ways," and sometimes, we're even unaware of how we come across. I've got what some folks might call a "focused face," and I've learned that my wife can read it like a book. So now, she has full permission to speak up if she sees that face come out, so I can be present and listen. Understand this: even if you don't intend something in a certain way, if your partner perceives it that way, you need to find a way to change that perception.

Remember that, in 1 Corinthians 9, Paul told us that he became all things to all men. In other words, he changed how he acted and presented things to different groups in different ways in an effort to reach them. He specified that he didn't compromise God's Word; he just understood that people's experiences, culture, or age can change how they hear what is being said. Sometimes, you just need to change what you say or do or how you say or do it. Sometimes, they need to simply understand that it is a peculiarity to you. Most of the time, it is a combination of both! So not only do we need to have grace in our speech, but we need to press into grace for the hearing as well.

☀ *Put Actions to Your Faith* ☀

Some of the action steps we put in place were making time together first thing in the morning and last thing at night a priority. When I am traveling, we wake up a little earlier or stay awake a little longer so that we can FaceTime for at least a minute or two to talk. When that isn't possible, we at least send text messages asking how the other person is doing. We also make a point after a disagreement that brought up emotions to ask the other person afterward if there would have been a better way to bring it up or word it that could have helped ease the conversation. Then, we do our best to put that into play in our next discussion.

Talking about the peace and love of God in marriage is wonderful, but you have to live it out. Put those words into action. That might mean saying, "Hey, we're going to come out of this better and stronger," even before you feel it. And finish the conversation, no matter what, with, "I'm here, and I'm listening. We're a team, and we are doing this together!" Keep planting those seeds of love, peace, and kindness, and watch what God can do.

Marriage is a journey. It's going to take time, it's going to take patience, and it's going to take words that speak life into each other. And remember, nothing's too small for God to handle or too large for Him to fix. Y'all got this—together.

To watch us speaking about this topic on our broadcast, scan the QR code below or type in:

https://davidweeter.org/broadcast/communicate/

CHAPTER

4

Dealing with Differences

Building a Rock-Solid Foundation for Your Marriage

A lot of what you'll see in this chapter comes from Biblical wisdom that's worked in our own lives, taking us from rough patches to a life of real joy and strength together. Whether your marriage feels like it's in a dry desert or a beautiful oasis, these principles can breathe life back into it and take it all the way to days of Heaven on Earth! Now, don't misunderstand us at all; there will always be opportunities to overcome and grow. We are not talking about a life of floating from one cloud to another.

Let's remember the foundation scripture that gets right to the heart of God's promise for us, regardless of where we are now. Isaiah 43:19 says, "Behold, I will do a new thing; now it shall spring forth. Shall you not know it? I will even make a way in the wilderness and rivers in the desert." In simple terms, God promises a path, even when everything around you feels barren and broken. And that's good news for us all. Because no matter what area of our life we are talking about, God offers new beginnings.

Think about it—God doesn't just watch us struggle. He actively makes ways where we think none exist. But we have to be open to seeing it. That word "behold" in Isaiah essentially means, "Look here! Pay attention!" So whatever mess we're in, He's there, making a way, even when it feels like we're at our end.

☀ *Peace Like a River, Not Just Calm Water* ☀

Another part of the foundation for us is 2 Thessalonians 3:16: "Now may the Lord of Peace Himself give you peace at all times and in every way." That's a big promise! And here's the thing—it doesn't just mean "peace" as in a quiet house. Nope, this peace is about being whole, like when you finally get all the pieces of a puzzle to fit together. In other words, it's "nothing missing, nothing broken." Imagine that for your marriage. God's will is for us to experience this type of wholeness, not because we're perfect, but because He loves us and desires that wholeness in our lives.

☀ *Embracing New Beginnings— and Breaking Them In* ☀

But how do we walk this out in our relationships, especially when differences keep tripping us up? That's where patience and a willingness to change come in. And, believe us, change is essential. If you're holding onto old ways or refusing to adjust, you're going to keep hitting the same walls. It's like the saying goes: "The only person who likes change is a baby with a dirty diaper"— and they'll even fight you about changing it, too!

You know, that was one *hot* topic back when I used to talk about needing to change. Right there in the thick of it—the worst parts—you'd hear folks saying, "Well, I'm like God. I change not." And sure enough, if you *were* like God, you'd be right. But let's be real: none of us are God, are we?

See, your spirit is made in God's image, and there is no doubt about that. But your mind? Well, that's got a long, long way to go before it gets anywhere near fully renewed into that image. That whole "I change not" thing only applies when you've reached perfection— and let's be honest, ain't a single one of us got there yet!

The Old Testament had a name for that kind of stubbornness. God called it "stiff-necked," like a mule that just won't budge. Quit being so stiff-necked and hard-hearted, y'all! God said He'd give us a heart of flesh—soft, pliable, ready to be molded. That means we *can* change, and sometimes we *need* to change.

Now, don't get me wrong, there *are* things you stand your ground on, no matter what. When it comes to sickness, disease, or the devil himself, you don't budge an inch. God's will is for everybody to be healthy and whole. That's a fact. And the one who steals your health, who comes to steal, kill, destroy, and wreak havoc? He is our enemy, and he has been defeated. That part never changes. That's a constant, but we, as people, need to be willing to change and grow. Sometimes, we must let go of that stubbornness and let God soften our hearts.

And let me just tell you, when you finally let God do a work in your marriage, things can change—and they can change quickly. But, just like with a new pair of boots, you still have to break them in even if they fit well. That's how it was for us, anyway. We got our new start, but there was a stretch of getting used to each other in this new way and learning to trust the process. If you're ready to lean into something new, just keep in mind it's gonna take a little work.

☀ *Understanding the Differences* ☀

Now, I've got to say that when discussing differences, if you're hoping to change your spouse, just go ahead and put that idea out of your head. It ain't happening. Change, especially in marriage, is a two-way street. When you're both willing to look honestly at your habits and hang-ups, that's when real transformation happens. If one person is ready to grow, but the other isn't, things become much harder. But when both people are committed to working on themselves—and relying on God to make the rough spots smooth—that's where breakthroughs happen.

But here's the good news: those little quirks and habits that might drive you crazy? They could be just the thing to balance you out. This starts with recognizing that your spouse's unique traits and tendencies aren't flaws; they're strengths that can benefit your relationship. Psalm 139 says that we are "fearfully and wonderfully made." God knew the qualities he had put in each of us before we were born. Now, we have to do the hard part of acknowledging those qualities. We know that's easier said than done. Lynn and I had to learn this the hard way.

Now, let me tell you something about communication. The way you communicate right now? That's been shaped by everything you've been through since you were born. Your family, your culture, your ethnicity—all those things come together to influence *how* you talk and *what* level of communication you achieve.

Did you know that because of differences in background and personality, someone can say something, and the person listening can hear the exact opposite of what was intended to be communicated? It definitely can and does happen often!

And let's be honest, God's got a really good sense of humor about it. He puts together people who are different. Usually, He'll pair you up with someone who's got a whole other set of experiences and ways of looking at the world. Maybe it's to help us grow, but one thing is for sure: it sure keeps things interesting!

For a long time, I thought we needed to agree on *everything* and that Lynn ought to see the world exactly like I did. Well, that's not how God designs it. There's a big difference between being in agreement and being carbon copies of each other. I tended to want Lynn to match my thinking, word for word, 100% of the time.

I'm what you might call "direct"—let's cut to the chase and get it done. Lynn? She's kind and likes to keep the peace. Early on, these differences could've gotten under our skin, but instead, we've learned to lean into them. I'll tell you this: if Lynn were exactly like me, it'd be like me being married to...well, me. She pointed out to me one time that if we were exactly the same, I would be going to bed every night with an older bearded guy! That's not a pretty picture, I assure you!

> *God put us here to balance each other out.*

In marriage, it's tempting to think, "If only they'd think like I do, things would be smoother." But God didn't put us here to be exact copies of each other. He put us here to balance each other out. Once we saw that, it changed things for us. Lynn's gentleness softened my rough edges, and maybe I added a little boldness to her kindness. Let's learn to celebrate these differences. Physically, emotionally, and spiritually, we're not meant to be exact copies of one another. When God brings two people together, they often have different backgrounds, perspectives, and strengths, all designed to complement each other.

Differences don't have to be battle zones. They can be a blessing. Lynn's got a gift for hospitality that'll put anyone at ease. Me? I'm more of a "get down to business" type. Put those together, and we make a good team. She brings people together to try to make sure the plan works for everyone, which can take more time, and I help keep things moving along. And that's a massive part of what God's after in marriage—two people using their strengths to bless each other and build each other up.

Remember this: when you're in covenant together, you are not compromising and losing out; you are collaborating, building up, and winning!

Sure, we don't agree on everything. And that's alright. But when we stop trying to change each other and start focusing on what each of us brings to the table, we realize we've got something strong, and we wouldn't trade it for the world.

☀ *Living with the Fruit of the Spirit* ☀

While we're learning to appreciate these qualities, we're also recognizing that patience is essential and here's a handy little verse that'll do wonders in your marriage in this area! It's in Galatians 5:22-23 and talks about the "fruit of the Spirit": love, joy, peace, patience, kindness, goodness, faithfulness, gentleness, and self-control. We know that's a mouthful. But take a minute to think about how each one of those qualities could help you communicate better, argue fairer, and just plain enjoy each other more.

But here's the catch: we can't muster up all that goodness on our own. We've gotta lean on the Holy Spirit to help us walk in love and patience because—let's be real—some days, we don't feel all that loving or patient. But when we ask God to help us, He shows up. And those fruit? They start growing. Little by little, they help us see things from the other person's perspective. If you're trying to tackle relationship challenges without God's help, it's going to be a tough road. But when you invite Him into the process, His spirit enables us to walk in love, patience, and understanding in ways we never could on our own.

If you are not born again or have not received the baptism of the Holy Spirit, please join us in praying the prayers at the end of this book. You need His help in these things!

☀ *Staying Open to God's Plan* ☀

With these things in place, if you're open to it, God'll use your spouse to show you things you wouldn't see otherwise. We know He's done that for us. There've been times when Lynn's insight helped me see a whole different perspective, one I never would've come to on my own. And it's not always easy to hear, especially when I'm set in my ways, but it's good. There were times when Lynn's perspective challenged me to open my eyes to something I hadn't considered. When we're willing to listen and see the other's viewpoint, God can work through both of us in ways that strengthen our relationship. God's got a way of working through our differences to build us up, not tear us down.

We must allow the Holy Spirit to reveal these things to us as he did to me in that church service we discussed in chapter 2. He told me, "You're not listening to her (Lynn). You need to be listening to her. I'm talking to you through her." That was to my advantage, but I'd seen it as a disadvantage. I had been seeing it as something that was trying to get me off track when, in reality, it was the opposite. It was something that the Lord was trying to use to get me on track to where we, as a couple and ministry, needed to go. This is also a good place to point out that a personality characteristic in and

> *When you're facing differences, it's helpful to see them as assets rather than obstacles.*

of itself is not bad. Tenacity and stubbornness are the same characteristics. However, it should be the tenacity of saying, "We WILL work through this together." versus the stubbornness of refusing to change or see a different viewpoint.

When you're facing differences, it's helpful to see them as assets rather than obstacles. For instance, I have the gift of focus and determination, while Lynn brings a gentle, nurturing approach. On my own, I might miss important emotional cues, while Lynn might overlook certain details without my perspective. Together, our strengths balance out. And, of course, that doesn't mean we agree on everything, but we're able to support each other's growth.

I really like an example that Lynn brought out one time based on scripture. She said if the whole body was a hand, it wouldn't get much done. And even within the hand, you have fingers and a thumb, which cause an opposing grip. The fingers are saying you are supposed to press down, but the thumb is saying you have to press up. Those are opposing viewpoints, but if the fingers don't do their part and the thumb doesn't do its part, you can't grip anything or get anything done.

When people are unwilling to see different perspectives in order to see the whole picture, it's not good! I've seen small wars about things that the scripture says. For example, in Mark's account of the gospel, he's talking about a leper who comes to Jesus. Listen to what he says in Mark 1:40, "and there came a leper to him, beseeching him and kneeling down to Him and saying unto him, If thou wilt, thou can make me clean." One person may be of the mindset that the leper knelt down. That is what this verse says; that is precisely what it says and only what it says. To this person, it can be no other way.

Someone else may be reading this account in Luke 5:12, "And it came to pass when he was in a certain city, behold a man full of leprosy who, seeing Jesus, fell on his face and besought him, saying, Lord, if thou will, thou can make me clean." The person reading this account says the leper fell on his face, while the person reading Mark's account says, "That can't be right because the scripture says he fell to his knees!" Neither one is willing to change their perspective and because of that, neither one is seeing the WHOLE picture.

Use your mind's eye and imagine this: Jesus is standing there, and this man with leprosy runs up to him and falls to his knees on his way down to the ground, ending up face down at Jesus' feet. NOW you have the whole picture! Too often, we insist that our way is the only way, and we don't see what the other person is seeing; we don't see how those two things can meld together.

So, as you go on, don't sweat those differences. Embrace them. God put you together with your spouse for a reason, quirks and all. Pray together, ask Him to show you how your differences can make each other better, and trust that He's got big plans for you both.

To watch us speaking about this topic on our broadcast, scan the QR code below or type in:

https://davidweeter.org/broadcast/dealing-with-differences

True Repentance

———

There's something I heard once—I think maybe it was Brother Keith Moore who'd pray it before every service—that really stuck with me. He'd ask God to help him speak the Word accurately but also prayed that everyone listening would hear it just as accurately.

When we talk about communication, we're not just talking about words flying back and forth; we're talking about accurate understanding. This kind of connection takes more than just speaking or hearing the words— it's about truly getting the message. Imagine if I say "dog," and immediately, you picture the pet you had as a kid, but someone else in the room pictures their big ol' Labrador. Without details, we're all left with our own ideas. But if I say, "a 60-pound black shaggy dog with a cropped tail and a slight limp," we're all seeing the same thing, aren't we? Sometimes, you have to clarify and get specific. That's the power of clear, intentional communication. That's what we are going to do as we go into this chapter on true repentance.

When we share our own story, it's not to point out our struggles but to show how God restored our marriage. We're going to get very specific about some things, especially when it comes to real, "godly sorrow" and the difference between feeling bad and actually changing our ways. We'll start with some scripture, get into what happened with us, and then explain how it all unfolded in two weekends.

Now, don't get the idea that real and significant change always takes forever because it doesn't. When God moves, He doesn't mess around—He's efficient. In our case, He did a complete restoration in less than two months, from the point of separation and divorce papers being filed to complete restoration. And let me tell you, that was nothing short of a miracle. Our son even told me it would take a full-on "Road to Damascus experience" for his mom not to go through with the divorce. Well, God pulled that off! Now, that wasn't just luck or coincidence; that was God at work, plain and simple.

☀ *What Repentance Looks Like* ☀

Let's talk about true, genuine repentance. Repentance isn't just about feeling bad or saying sorry; it's about turning away from what's wrong and moving toward something better. It's like Peter when he denied Jesus three times. The moment he heard that rooster crow and realized what he'd done, he felt deep sorrow. But later, Jesus was

> *When God moves,*
> *He doesn't*
> *mess around—*
> *He's efficient.*

able to restore him. This story teaches us that godly sorrow—the kind that leads us to repentance—is different from worldly sorrow, which often leaves us stuck in guilt or shame.

Sometimes, we've been taught that repentance means burying ourselves in guilt. Too often, we've got people carrying around the wrong kind of sorrow, the worldly kind. But genuine repentance doesn't mean your mistakes forever condemn you. It means changing your heart and your actions to match what God desires. That's the sorrow and repentance Paul was talking about in 2 Corinthians 7:10.

"For godly sorrow worketh repentance to salvation not to be repented of: but the sorrow of the world worketh death." 2 Corinthians 7:10 *KJV*

"For godly grief and the pain God is permitted to direct, produce a repentance that leads and contributes to salvation and deliverance from evil, and it never brings regret; but worldly grief (the hopeless sorrow that is characteristic of the pagan world) is deadly [breeding and ending in death]." 2 Corinthians 7:10 *AMPC*

The worldly sorrow is what was working in Judas and ended in death.

Godly sorrow gets you closer to God; it's not about heaping shame on yourself. When you're in a pit of condemnation—still grieving something from way back—that's worldly sorrow. It's not from God, and it doesn't lead to life; it just keeps you stuck. In other words, the kind of sorrow that leads to change doesn't leave us feeling broken; it leads us to a fresh start.

The Power of Putting Safeguards in Place

Repentance isn't just about saying you're sorry; it's about taking real action to prevent the same mistakes from happening again. For example, if a pastor finds themselves slipping up in certain situations, real repentance means setting boundaries to avoid those pitfalls. This could mean making sure they're never alone with someone of the opposite sex or taking accountability measures.

Sometimes, it's not obvious what needs to be done. Take it to the Lord and ask Him. It might be a simple word from Him that marks your thinking. I'm reminded of a time in our relationship when Lynn seemed to be irritated with me most of the time. She told me later that when she took that to the Lord, He told her that whenever she was mad at me for more than two or three things simultaneously, it wasn't me; it was her. Now, I am fully aware of my capabilities and am pretty confident that I could possibly be doing more than two or three things simultaneously that would cause her irritation, but who am I to argue with the Lord?! Praise God for his intervention.

For each of us, repentance might mean different actions. If you find yourself tempted in certain areas—

whether it's unhealthy habits, anger, or anything else—set up the safeguards you need. Sometimes, that means avoiding certain places certain people, or even using tools that block access to things that can lead to sin. Real repentance changes how we act. Change your patterns, your surroundings, and your boundaries.

When Sorrow Leads to Change

Now, let's get brutally honest. Repentance isn't just about being sorry you got caught! Kids are experts at this one, right? They'll say, "Sorry," but it's only because they're caught, not because they're actually ready to change. Adults aren't much different sometimes. You can say I'm sorry all day long, but if you're just trying to find a better way to hide it, you're fooling yourself, not God.

God sees straight through our hearts. We can make excuses to others, even to ourselves, but He knows the truth. If we're just setting up ways not to get caught, it's only a matter of time before the consequences hit. Like Paul said, "God is not mocked; for whatsoever a man soweth, that shall he also reap" (Galatians 6:7).

Godly sorrow leads to a real turnaround. You don't keep running around in the same circles or making the same excuses. You can fool people for a while, maybe, but in the end, you're just setting yourself up for disaster.

I had to learn that myself. I had to get to a point where my heart was changed—not from condemnation but conviction.

True repentance isn't about being sorry we got caught. It's about a genuine, deep sorrow that leads us to turn away from harmful actions. When we think of the difference between Peter and Judas, we see this clearly. Judas felt sorrow for his betrayal, but it didn't lead him to change. Instead, it led to despair. But Peter's sorrow led to transformation, and Jesus was able to restore him.

If you feel guilt or regret, confess it to God. True repentance isn't about condemnation; it's about recognizing what's gone wrong and allowing God to guide you in a new direction!

Remember our foundation scriptures?

"Behold, I will do a *new thing;* now it shall spring forth; shall ye not know it? I will even make a way in the wilderness *and* rivers in the desert." Isaiah 43:19 *KJV*

"Now the Lord of peace himself give you peace always by all means. The Lord be with you all." 2 Thessalonians 3:16 *KJV*

Godly sorrow leads to repentance, and true repentance makes those scriptures a reality in your life and marriage!

☀ *The Journey Forward—* *Willingness and Forgiveness* ☀

Years before our big turning point, God had been working on me, but I wasn't moving fast enough. I was still holding onto my own way, holding out, even though deep down, I wanted to be better. I remember telling God, "Lord, I'm willing to be willing." I couldn't see the whole path forward, but that was my first step— getting willing.

It took a series of challenging situations and some rocky times before I finally got there. We had a year of nonstop challenges. Stuff was coming at us from every angle–personally, financially, and in the ministry. For a very long time, the devil had been working on setting us up for a fall, and it was reaching a boiling point. We were both struggling. But God, even in those moments, had a plan, and He told me I had to be at a specific service, at a particular church, on a particular date. I almost didn't go, I'll be honest, but I showed up. And let me tell you, God moved.

> *True repentance can be instant. However, rebuilding trust is proven out over time through actions, not just intentions.*

I had no idea it would be the turning point for me, but it felt like God reached down inside me and gave me a new heart during that service. I don't know how else to say it other than I felt born again, again! It was such a massive and immediate change! A fresh start, full of clarity and purpose! But that's not where the work ended. Even though I had this new heart and new commitment, the circumstances in my life hadn't changed overnight. Our journey wasn't over. There was still work to do.

Even after this happened, Lynn still wasn't sure. She had announced our separation, was in a different state, and limited our communication, and there I was, a changed man, trying to find my way back to her. It wasn't easy, and she needed to see genuine, godly sorrow in my actions, not just my words. True repentance can be instant. However, rebuilding trust is proven out over time through actions, not just intentions. Where Lynn was concerned, after she did see the change, she realized she was going to have to walk in forgiveness.

If there's one thing we all know, forgiveness isn't always easy. It's a choice we make to let go of resentment and bitterness, even when it's hard. But here's the thing: forgiveness is the key to real freedom. Without it, we're chained to past hurts, unable to embrace God's peace and purpose fully.

In our own journey, we faced many challenges. Our son told me it would take a "Road to Damascus" kind of experience for Lynn to even think about reconciliation. And you know what? God did just that in one weekend. It was a miracle that reminded us of the power of forgiveness and restoration.

In the upcoming chapters, we'll get deeper into what happened after that service. We'll talk about how God started to rebuild our lives and our marriage from the ground up and how each step brought us closer to the relationship God had planned for us. We hope you'll stick around because this isn't just our story. It's about the power of God to take brokenness and turn it into something new. We can't do it alone, but with God, even the most hopeless situation can turn around.

To watch us speaking about this topic on our broadcast, scan the QR code below or type in:

https://davidweeter.org/broadcast/true-repentance/

Getting the Fear Out

☀ *Getting the Fear Out* ☀

"Your zeal, passion, and determination mixed with great fear has caused great damage, but I am a greater God." -Word from the Lord to David.

One of the most powerful things we can do in our lives—whether in our relationships, work, or ministry—is to root out fear and reclaim our path with a clear mind and heart. For many of us, fear can slip in unnoticed, disguised as diligence or even as a drive to do good work. The problem? Fear, left unchecked, can start steering us in directions we'd never intentionally choose, often creating problems rather than solving them. This chapter takes us through understanding and eliminating fear, finding love in our actions, and maintaining a compassionate approach, even in the face of hardship.

☀ *Recognizing Fear in Our Lives* ☀

Do you remember that church service the Lord directed me to attend? We have already talked about what He said to me regarding being stiff-necked, hard-hearted, and basically not listening to Lynn, where He was trying to get things across to me through her. Now, it is time for the rest of the story. Then He said, "I commend you for your zeal, passion, and determination to stay true to your calling and the message." Stop right there. Those parts, the zeal, the passion, and the determination, were correct. He commended me for those things.

Nevertheless, He continued, "However, you allowed it to be mixed with great fear, fear that you would go off course, fear that a false doctrine would get in undetected and veer you off course, as you have seen so many others do. Your zeal, passion, and determination, mixed with great fear, has caused great damage. But I am a greater God." And then He continued, and listen to this very closely, particularly if you are a minister in the fivefold ministry of any kind if you're in helps ministry, etc. But it also applies if you're in a secular job because you might be afraid of losing your job, or you're fearful of being laid off, losing your benefits, etc. But especially for those of you who are involved in ministry, listen closely to what He said next, "in your fearful determination to keep out incorrect or distracting words that would take you off course, you have kept out the very words that would put you on course to the fullness of the manifestation of your calling through the very person I gave you to trust. The fear that drove you to keep out anything that would take you to the right or to the left also kept out the very thing that would take you up!" Yes, there are situations out there where people have gone off course and they've destroyed their ministries, or they've destroyed people in the wake of their ministries because they let incorrect doctrine get in. Yes, it happens. No, that is no reason to be afraid of it. The passion and the zeal were good, but the fear gave Satan entrance to work through all of it, and it kept me from the very thing that we needed in our lives and ministry to take us up to the next level.

Fear often masquerades as other qualities we value. For instance, diligence and excellence are great virtues, but sometimes, they become cloaks for deeper worries, such as the fear of failure or the making of mistakes. I spent years living without realizing that my own diligence was sometimes powered by an undercurrent of fear—a fear that I'd make the wrong choice or drift off course. Yet, when we act from fear rather than faith, our path often narrows, limiting our potential and diminishing our impact. It's critical to identify where fear might be operating in your life. Once you see it, you can begin to get rid of it.

The Damage Fear Can Cause

Fear, even when hidden, can cause damage not just to us but to the people around us. Faith and fear are reciprocal forces. Faith and fear are the same spiritual force going in opposite directions. This can be easily seen in the fact that your fear of a dangerous animal is your faith in that animal's ability to harm you. Just as faith attracts the things of God to your life, fear enables the devil to get in and mess things up. In my life, I came to realize that my own drive, zeal, and determination—while good qualities—had been mixed with a fear that I could go astray and that false ideas could sneak in and disrupt my life and work. But in my fear-driven determination to stay on track, I had blocked out the very words and wisdom that would have helped guide me correctly. I was clinging so tightly to control that I wasn't open to the support and guidance available to me.

Imagine for a moment you're in a relationship, or even a job for that matter, constantly afraid of failure or rejection. Maybe you're so scared of disappointing your partner or boss that you end up bottling up concerns or doing things with which you don't agree. Over time, these decisions can strain the relationship, creating walls rather than building trust. The same thing happened to me. I was so fearful of veering off course that I inadvertently shut out the very things that would have taken me to the next level. Whether you're talking about the ministry, a job, or a relationship, it's the same story: fear messes with your mind, holding you back from seeing things clearly. It twists good intentions until they're nothing but a shadow of what they're meant to be.

> *Fear often masquerades as other qualities we value.*

☀ *How Love Casts Out Fear* ☀

One of the most transformative realizations came from the understanding that perfect love casts out fear (1 John 4:18). We often talk about love in its many forms —patience, kindness, compassion—but sometimes, we miss the "perfect" part of love, which drives out fear completely my own journey, I discovered that fear-driven actions ultimately lead to distress, as fear itself is a form of torment. I came to see that only in love can faith truly flourish.

I had to question my own understanding of love and reflect on what it really meant. I'd heard about love and even studied love, but the thing is, I hadn't let go of my old "tough love" approach. True love isn't about having harsh boundaries all the time or tough love at every turn. Scripture doesn't talk about "tough love" the way we think it does. It speaks of compassion, gentleness, and kindness. I used to think I was loving in a way that would make others better or stronger, but I came to realize that real love doesn't always need to be hard. For love to be transformative, it must be communicated in a way that others receive and understand.

☀ *Understanding Love Languages* ☀

We know this in marriage, too, right? We're all trying to do our best, trying to show love. But if you're showing love the way *you* feel it rather than the way *they* feel it, well, you're kind of wasting your time. I mean, not totally, but let's be honest, mostly. I learned that love means communicating it in a way that actually reaches the person you love, not just in a way that feels "right" to you. When I found out how important that is, it changed everything between us.

Part of loving others well is understanding their love language. Each of us expresses and receives love differently, and knowing the love language of those around us can make all the difference. For example, Lynn's love language is quality time and physical touch, and we spent years in situations where those were hard to come by. Let me remind you of the days when I was traveling all the time, spending hundreds of nights a year in hotels. And let me tell you, FaceTime doesn't cut it! I thought that everything else would fall into place because I was out working hard and doing my part. But I hadn't paused to think about what she truly needed to feel loved and valued. We didn't put any real thought into figuring out a solution; we just let it be what it was. We never stopped to say, "You know what, God? You brought us together, and you can help us work this out, no matter how big or small."

If you don't know about love languages, I encourage you to learn about them. Knowing the love language of your spouse, children, or friends allows you to reach out to them in ways that mean the most to them. It's not enough to love in the way we think is right; we have to love in ways that others can feel and understand.

☀ *Standing Firm in Faith, Not Fear* ☀

Another important realization I came to was how much fear influences our actions in all areas of life, not just in our relationships. Even when we think we're standing firm, we need to be sure we're doing so from a place of faith and not fear. Fear of failure, of losing loved ones, or even of not measuring up in our own eyes can sneak in and overshadow our faith. Scripture reminds us not to focus on temporary things but on the eternal. If we dwell on every small fear or passing challenge, it will only grow. Instead, let's focus on the truths that don't change.

Sometimes, this means revisiting past experiences and recognizing the small cracks, the moments when we acted from fear, not love. It's not about dwelling on regret but rather about learning to make different choices moving forward.

Looking back, we can see how Satan got into those tiny cracks. Little things, those little misunderstandings, they add up. I had my fears about being too involved or not enough, and she had hers about needing too much or too little. Communication, or the lack of it, became our own stumbling block, and it's probably the same for a lot of folks out there. We were both afraid of being a burden to each other and instead of tackling it head-on, we just dealt with it however we could.

I used to think I was showing love by taking care of her, by being the steady, reliable one. But that steady love she needed didn't come in the form of grand gestures or fixing things—it was just simple time, simple words, a little patience. And that's where God's Word on love really comes through. Love isn't just big sacrifices or mighty gestures; it's the small, tender moments, too, even the ones that don't come naturally to us.

From Lynn's perspective, throughout her entire life, she has received a lot of attention for being low maintenance. She could always entertain herself as a child and never needed much "coddling." Once we were married, I also bragged to other guys and praised her for being low-maintenance. That reinforced her not wanting to ask for help or attention because she didn't want to lose that low-maintenance status. She tried to do everything that was asked of her; she has a reputation for being able to do or figure out how to do anything. A reputation not wholly undeserved. Because of this, she ended up pushing herself beyond her ability and limits, trying to make everyone, especially me, happy. In reality, the extreme drive was because of fear. She believed that she was pushing in this area to try to make me happy, when in reality, as a man, I wanted to minister to her by helping her with these things where I could. This goes back to the lack of communication being a huge stumbling block that allowed the devil to get in and use fear to create more issues. Lynn had a difficult time going back and forth; she would need to be extremely independent when I was traveling, but when I was back home, I would want to come in and fix things and take care of things. Because of our lack of communication, Satan was able to exploit the situation, and Lynn would think, "What are you doing? This is my domain." On top of that, there was a fear that if we addressed it, then it would lead to even more problems. So, we simply didn't deal with it at all, and fear continued to magnify the problem.

Right here, we want to address a strategic tactic of the devil. He has always attempted to twist the Word of God. He did so with Jesus in the wilderness. He has been doing it since the very beginning when he tried to tell Eve what God had said. In this case, he attempted to use James 3:16: "For where envying and strife *is,* there *is* confusion and every evil work." For many, he has convinced them that disagreements are the same as strife. Because of

> *Once you let God come into the middle of that fear and insecurity, things change.*

that, after just a couple of back-and-forth exchanges, I would simply stop talking because I didn't want there to be strife. In reality, the strife was still there, and I had stopped the process of getting rid of it.

Now, here's the lesson in all this: once you let God come into the middle of that fear and insecurity, things change. In fact, it's like He pours love into those cracks and crevices, filling up every gap fear had snuck into. And you get stronger, not because you're doing everything perfectly, but because you're doing it together with God's help.

Remember what God told me, and don't ever lose sight of this: ★"Your zeal, passion, and determination mixed with great fear have caused great damage, but I am a greater God."★ No matter what damage fear has done, no matter what it's twisted up in your life, He is bigger. And He's a God of grace. Where sin abounds, grace abounds even more.

☀ *Moving Forward Together* ☀

Love, faith, and courage go hand in hand. It takes courage to love deeply, to communicate openly, and to be vulnerable in relationships. Fear often makes us put up walls or shy away from conversations that could bring us closer together. By flushing out fear and focusing on love, we open up space for greater understanding and stronger connections.

In any relationship, but especially your marriage, take time to communicate. Your marriage should be a covenant-safe place to express your fears and listen to your partner's, too. Share your goals, and support each other's dreams. And if you feel afraid or uncertain, remember: there is a way forward, and you don't have to face it alone. Where there has been pain or misunderstanding, there can also be healing and unity. And if fear starts to creep back in, don't hesitate to take a stand on your faith and remind yourself of the grace that surrounds you.

In the end, our path becomes clearest not when we're fear-driven but when we're love-guided. Fear has a way of shrinking our vision and our potential. Love, on the other hand, expands our hearts, opens new doors, and keeps us moving forward. As we continue on, may we always choose love over fear, trusting that no matter what we face, we are equipped to overcome it with courage, compassion, faith, and the Word of God.

We can't look at our present circumstances, because that will breed fear. We have to look at the Word, walking it out through love. That's why we begin these chapters with those foundation scriptures, because that's the end goal. That's the objective. That's God's will. These temporary circumstances, this desert, this wilderness, are temporary. It is subject to change. We look at the eternal (the Word) and then we have to walk it out.

So, let me wrap this up by saying this: love covers a multitude of things. And it's what makes faith stronger. We need to take a moment here to address a significant issue, not only in marriage and family but in the entire spectrum of life. Galatians 5:6 says, "Faith works by love." When you study that out, it actually says that faith becomes efficient, effective, and mighty through the channel of love. As Christians, and particularly Christian husbands and Christian wives, the Scripture tells us that we are to live our entire lives by faith. Consequently, when you focus on maximizing love, your faith becomes very strong, which indeed produces a wonderful life.

If you're walking in love, there's no room for fear. So don't let fear run your life. Don't let it dictate your ministry, your relationships, or your purpose. Lean into God's love, that perfect love that casts out fear, and watch how things shift in ways you could never plan yourself. That's how you walk out of fear and into faith for good.

To watch us speaking about this topic on our broadcast, scan the QR code below or type in:

https://davidweeter.org/broadcast/get-the-fear-out/

The Road to Damascus Weekend

☀ *The Road to Damascus Weekend* ☀

This chapter is going to be a little different and a little longer than the others. Up to now, we've been sharing bits and pieces of our story, laying out lessons from the Bible, and talking about the ways we've messed up, learned, and grown in our marriage. But this chapter? This one is about the turning point—that "Road to Damascus" weekend that changed everything for us.

So, grab your coffee, settle in, and let's get into it.

☀ *A Messy Foundation* ☀

In almost every chapter, we've gone over these passages. Isaiah 43:19: "Behold, I will do a new thing; now it shall spring forth." And let me tell you, when God says He'll make rivers in the desert, He means it— even in the driest, most tangled-up mess of a relationship. Second Thessalonians 3:16 says, "Now may the Lord of peace Himself grant you His peace at all times and in every way." And let me tell you, when peace shows up in the middle of chaos, that's when things start to change.

But our marriage wasn't looking much like those verses at that time. There was a time when it felt like we were speaking different languages. Differences that once felt exciting and fresh had become sources of frustration and miscommunication. Like many couples, we found ourselves caught in patterns where misunderstandings overshadowed the appreciation we once had for each other's unique perspectives. We have already talked about how things between us had hit rock bottom. Misunderstandings, not appreciating each other's differences, downright stubbornness—it had all piled up. And, well, she had filed for divorce. I was gutted. The hurt went deep because, even though I knew I'd made a lot of mistakes and there was a lot of work to do, I knew the change God had made in me and had never even considered that she would really, actually, file for divorce. That was the reality we were in. She had requested little to no contact, and I was left praying for a miracle.

What she didn't know was that the Lord had been working on me. He had sent me to that church service at just the right time, and He turned my heart upside down. But since we weren't talking much, she had no way to see it, which, let me tell you, was frustrating as all get out.

Truth be told, she didn't think I wanted her anymore. She had convinced herself that I wouldn't have chosen her if I could do it all over again. I would have picked someone more agreeable, someone who never challenged me. She thought I was looking for someone who'd say, "Yes, sir! You're so smart, so handsome. Whatever you say is gospel." And, in all honesty, I hadn't shown her any different. I was so focused on what I thought was right, what I thought God was leading me to do, that I completely missed what was happening in her heart. And in her mind, that meant there was no hope. Satan had actually convinced her that she was doing me a favor by giving me a way out of a marriage I didn't want to be in anymore.

I knew that wasn't true, but convincing her was another thing entirely. So, I took it to the Lord and prayed for something big. I prayed for a road-to-Damascus moment for her, something so clear that she couldn't deny the change in me.

☀ *A New Beginning* ☀

Well, hold up a minute. For clarity, let me back up, and bullet point the timeline of events leading up to this pivotal weekend:

- August 2: The Lord told me to attend a particular church service on August 16.

- August 15: We were in different states, had a significant fight on FaceTime, and she said we were now "separated."

- August 16: The Lord changed my heart in the church service He had told me to attend. It felt like being born again, again.

- September 14: I thought the change was so apparent that I told Lynn that if she didn't think the change was real, she should go ahead and file.

- September 15: Unbeknownst to me, she filed for divorce.

- September 18: I was served with divorce papers.

- September 27: Lynn had massive dental work done and hours under anesthesia. I was preaching out of town.

- October 1: Minutes before taking the platform to preach on the things she had been trying to get over to me for years, my phone lights up, and I see, via our home security cameras, my children helping my wife move her things out of our home.

On October 2, I returned home from my ministry trip, and my son came to me and said, "Dad, I don't know why. I don't know the reasoning, but I'm telling you right now that Mom has to see that finalized divorce. She has to have it in her hand before she will ever consider the possibility of a future relationship. I'm not saying that God can't do it, but I'm telling you it would take a Road to Damascus experience for mom to change her mind and not see the finalization of this divorce all the way through."

Although this was not necessarily encouraging, I kept putting the pressure on my covenant. I would remind myself and the Lord, "Father, You are a covenant-keeping God. You are the head of this marriage covenant. Now, keep this covenant!" I also spent a whole lot of time that week praying in the spirit and listening for instructions.

Now, we already had a plan in place for the coming weekend. I was supposed to meet her halfway between home and where she was to pick up our elderly dog and go right back home. No extra visiting, no unnecessary talking. But the Lord put something on my heart. I knew she had just been through that challenging dental procedure and was mentally and physically exhausted. She had previously mentioned that we needed to have a family financial discussion sometime soon and that it needed to be face-to-face. So I told her, "Why don't I just come all the way up, spend the night in my car if you are uncomfortable with me being in the house, and we'll go over the family finances like you wanted? That way, you don't have to drive all the way to meet me just to turn right around and go back." She agreed to let me come up for the weekend so we could go over things, but she was clear: there'd be no "visiting." Now, I had a glimmer of hope.

As we go through the story of this weekend, pay very close attention to how the Lord orchestrated everything step by step!

Our original plan: meet halfway, pick up the dog, go back. That would mean about 5 minutes together.

New plan: drive up in the morning, spend the afternoon/evening going over finances, spend the night, return the next morning. That would mean hours and hours together.

There were just a handful of my closest friends who knew what was going on because, during times like these, the last thing you need is a lot of people's doubt and unbelief about your situation being spoken into your life. You need people that you KNOW will be in faith with you for a victorious outcome. That being said, you better believe I got on the phone and told them all that I didn't know what they had previously planned for this weekend, but as of now, they were spending it in prayer for us!

So, I woke up early on Saturday morning and prepared for the trip. The Lord instructed me to put a sports coat and slacks in the car, so I did. I left at 6 a.m. and had about a six-hour drive, so I just started it out by praying in the spirit.

After about an hour and a half of praying in the spirit, I heard myself say this in English, "Father, I am asking You for such a tangible manifestation of Your love and Your presence that it will cause the walls to come down enough that Lynn can see this change that has taken place and that it would result in her 'Road to Damascus' experience this weekend!"

Apparently, that is what I had been praying out in the spirit, and now it came out in faith in English! After that, I just began praising God and thanking Him. That is exactly how this weekend will go!

Then, about ⅔ of the way up there, something completely unexpected happened. The Lord began speaking to me about something I hadn't thought of in years. I had grown up hearing it preached, "Don't you EVER sit in some unbelieving church and let doubt and unbelief be fed into your spirit!" Well, I took that very literally, and so, from the time we got together, I would not go to church with Lynn's family, and, of course, if I didn't go, she didn't go. She had come out of a very traditional denomination that didn't believe much beyond getting born again and then someday getting to go to Heaven. We did get married in that church, but we had not gone inside that church more than four or maybe five times in 30 years. Lynn had never complained about it to me at all, and we had not even mentioned it in years. Well, now the Lord was mentioning it!

The Lord said, "You were just plain wrong about that. You know how much family means to Pop. You know how much it would have meant to him to have his family with him in church, and you have denied him that for all these years. Lynn was born and raised in that church. She grew up with those people. You denied her the ability to go back and visit the people she grew up with for all those years. That church believes in Jesus and that He died for your sins. If your faith is so fragile and weak that you couldn't sit through a 45-minute, unbelieving message 2-3 times a year when you were in town, you really need to re-evaluate some things, and we have whole other issues we need to deal with! You were wrong, and when you get up there with Lynn, I want you to tell her you were wrong and apologize for it. No excuses or reasons. Just tell her you were wrong and apologize." Of course, my only response was, "Yes, sir."

I arrived at her dad's place (where she was living) just before noon. Her dad wanted the blackberry bushes pruned and wanted to oversee it, so we got him seated out there in a chair. We all visited while Lynn and I pruned the blackberry bushes. It struck me even then that, with all the distance between us, we still worked together like a fine-tuned machine when it came to things like that.

After that work was done, we went inside, and Lynn and I began making supper. We have always enjoyed cooking together, so it was natural. It also provided an excellent opportunity to start discussing things.

First of all, I did what the Lord told me and told her I was wrong about the church attendance. I apologized for it and asked if perhaps I could go with her and her dad to church the following day. I had no idea as I was saying it that this simple step the Lord orchestrated may very well have been the single biggest key to this weekend! She told me that I was welcome to come with them and return to Texas afterward. She told me later that one statement was what cracked the wall because I admitted I was wrong about it. I made no excuse for it but simply apologized and asked her to forgive me, AND it signaled that perhaps there had been a change because we had not even discussed that in years. She told me later that she had prepared herself to be courteous and professional in our discussions that weekend but was determined not to listen to anything I had to say regarding relationship things. For my part, now I knew why the Lord had me pack that sport coat and slacks, and now He had arranged for a few more hours together!

The next order of business during the conversation was for me to lay out a couple of things from a life and finance standpoint that she needed to know before our actual finance meeting. I wanted her to know that even if she did not get back together with me, I was willing to move up to where she was and get a job at Home Depot or somewhere just to be somewhere in the vicinity and that I was willing to roll up all the "business" of ministry and stick it on the shelf if need be. In short, nobody and nothing would ever come before her again except my personal relationship with Jesus. During all this time, she was just listening and processing what I was saying, but then, in the course of further conversation, she made me aware of a procedure her father was supposed to have on Monday morning.

I could tell there was something about this procedure that she was uncomfortable with, and I could put into action what I had just told her. I said, "Baby, there is nothing on my schedule that can't be canceled or rescheduled if need be. I would like to be here to support you through this procedure if you will allow me." She said she would have to pray about it, and after supper, she told me that she would appreciate my support if I would please stay through the procedure.

The steps of a righteous man are ordered by the Lord! Now, look at what the Lord did. He took what was supposed to be a 5-minute interaction at about noon on Saturday and extended it to a multiday, in-person interaction to allow Lynn more time to see the changes that had taken place back in August at that church service!

That night, Lynn said she was okay with me sleeping in one of the spare bedrooms. On a somewhat humorous note, but still applicable because it was yet one more thing that spoke to her about the change that had taken place in me, was the fact that I had offered to sleep in the SUV at night if she wasn't comfortable with me sleeping in the house. She knew that I despised the thought of sleeping in the car because I was forced to do it a few times when I was a child, so for me to offer it was a big thing!

The next morning, we all got up and went to church! I had a wonderful time just visiting with everyone and loving on people. I genuinely enjoyed myself.

When we got home from church, she and I went to the front porch swing to discuss the family finances. Other questions and conversations took place. By this time, she was very warily entertaining the fact that perhaps some kind of change had indeed taken place because of what she had heard and seen in my expressions and body language, not only in my interactions with her but also with the people at church, and so she had some questions.

I had anticipated and prepared answers to several questions, but then she asked one I had not expected. The question itself is not important. I was totally unprepared for it, so the answer was not "polished." I stumbled about in my response, and she began crying. Now I thought I had really messed up! I started quickly apologizing and trying to reassure her that, even if I had messed up that answer, I was very willing to learn more and to learn from her because she was so much better at these things than I was.

She started shaking her head, and when she was able to speak, she said, "No, that is exactly what I wanted to hear, and I could tell that it came from your heart." Then she reached out and took my hand. Now, to her, holding hands is an intimate thing, so you can rest assured that I was one thankful man at that point! I knew the Lord was working!

The next morning, we got up and took Pop to his procedure. Everything went perfectly, and we returned to his house. After we returned, he started to go into his room to use the restroom, and we headed back out to the front porch swing. Lynn apologized to him for not spending a lot of time visiting with him. He stopped in his tracks, came back out, and said, "I want you to hear this. I want both of you to hear this. What you are doing out there is far more important than visiting with me! Get to it!" Lynn has always been a "daddy's girl," and his opinion carried weight with her. I thought it was so special that the Lord even made sure to let Lynn know what her dad thought about us working things out.

Lynn and I went back out to the front porch swing. It has always been a special place for us. This time, though, we didn't talk much. We just spent time with each other, and pretty soon, she laid her head on my shoulder. Then, after a bit, she scrunched up on the swing and laid her head in my lap. It's a fairly small swing, though, so she looked uncomfortable. I said to her, "Sweetheart, if you are comfortable enough to lay your head in my lap, why don't we go inside and lay on your bed and let me hold you. We can leave the door open. I am not talking about any "funny business" here, just me holding you." You see, ever since we've been married, that has been our "safe place," our peaceful place. Dressed, undressed, it didn't matter—just holding each other. It's not sexual, but very intimate.

She replied, "Yes, that would be nice." So, we went in, and she faced away from me on the bed and just let me hold her. After a little bit, she began crying. She cried for several minutes and then turned toward me with her head on my chest and cried for a little longer. Then she quit, pulled back from me a little bit, looked me in the eyes, and said, "Will you love me forever, no matter what?" Without conscious thought about my response, I said, "Yes, I do, and I will." Then she said, "Will we always be equal partners together in life and ministry?" I responded, "Yes, I do, and I will."

With our eyes locked, she slightly nodded and then said, "OK, then from this moment forward, I will no longer pursue the divorce, and we are fully back together." On the outside, I remained calm and honored the weight and preciousness that the moment demanded, but on the inside, my heart was soaring to indescribable heights! The keeper of our covenant had just done the miraculous! He had just given Lynn her Road to Damascus experience!

She said, "I know there will be some things to walk out, and I don't know what all that will look like, but whatever it looks like, we will be doing it together."

Unfortunately, I needed to drive back to Texas just a few hours later to handle some family business the next day, but I think the car just slowed me down! I think I could have flown there just because of the joy I had!

As you can imagine, I replayed every step of the weekend many times on the drive back to Texas, and somewhere along the way, it dawned on me that her questions and my answers lying face-to-face together sounded a whole lot like wedding vows. One of the reasons that Lynn was so determined to see the divorce finalized was that she didn't want to "patch this mess up;" she wanted a brand new start.

The next day, Tuesday, we were visiting on FaceTime together, and I said, "Baby, I believe the Lord gave us a brand new marriage complete with vows; what do you think?" She laughed and said, "In responding to that, let me show you a picture that I

Don't ever think there is something too hard or big for God to handle.

drew about 2 hours before you got here on Saturday."
She showed me the picture that you can see on the
back cover of this book. I said it was beautiful, but was
it supposed to be a sunrise or a sunset? She laughed and
turned it over. At the top of the page, she had written
that very question just after she had drawn it. Then,
below that question, she wrote the Lord's immediate
response, "Yes. It is both." It's the sunset on the old and
the sunrise on the new.

And that happened two hours before our miracle
weekend together began!

God is a good God! He's a covenant-keeping God!
Don't ever think there is something too hard or big for
Him to handle. What He did for us, He can do for you!

To watch us speaking about this

topic on our broadcast, scan the
QR code below or type in:

https://davidweeter.org/broadcast/
the-testimony/

CHAPTER
8

Forgiveness

—

The Road to Damascus weekend was a glorious miracle in our lives. As we said, the Lord gave us a brand new marriage. Now is the time to press into continued growth and development. It would be similar to someone experiencing the glorious miracle of being born again. However, if that's all they ever did, they would not walk in the fullness of life that God intended for them. The final chapters deal with essential elements that helped us continue to walk out the victory God gave us.

Remember our instructions in Romans 12. It's one thing to be born again, but Romans 12:2 says that our lives are actually **transformed by the renewing** of our mind so that we may prove what is that good and acceptable and perfect will of God. In order for continued growth and victory, you have to continually **renew your mind** so that you do not "backslide" into old habits and patterns of thought that created the problems in the first place.

When relationships reach the brink—when trust is broken, hurt is deep, and separation seems like the only answer—it's easy to think all hope is lost. Lynn and I found ourselves in just that place. As you know, divorce wasn't just a distant concept; the papers were filed—it was becoming official. We were on the road to separation, both emotionally and practically. If you've ever been there, you know that you start grasping for anything steady when the foundation shakes. For us, we turned back to scripture. I leaned on "foundation scriptures"—passages that tell you God's plan can redeem any mess, but only if you're both willing to trust in that covenant. We were blessed enough to come back to that covenant, though not without some bumps and bruises. Through this storm, we learned something powerful: forgiveness isn't just a quick fix; it's a path that involves true change, faith, and a lot of humility.

In this chapter, we'll walk through the journey my wife and I took—from brokenness to wholeness—and explore how forgiveness goes beyond simply saying, "I'm sorry." It's about real change, accepting responsibility, and understanding the power of a covenant. If you're in a situation where forgiveness seems impossible, or if the idea of healing and wholeness feels like a distant dream, I invite you to dive into this chapter with an open heart.

In chapter 5, we explored repentance—not just saying sorry because you got caught, but real, deep repentance that leads to transformation. The reciprocal part of that is learning to forgive without requiring immediate change from the other person. True forgiveness is not contingent on the other person's actions; it's a personal decision to release resentment and trust God with justice and restoration.

☀ *Biblical Foundation for Forgiveness* ☀

Mark 11:25 commands us to forgive when we pray so that our Father in heaven may forgive us. That's a clear and direct instruction, but it can be incredibly difficult when we feel deeply wronged. "Well, you don't know what they did to me." You're right. I don't know your situation, but I do know that as long as you're walking in unforgiveness, the hurt continues to have power over you. Unforgiveness doesn't punish the other person—it keeps you in bondage.

Forgiveness was fully provided when Jesus went to the cross. Every imaginable or unimaginable sin was paid for. But if we refuse to forgive, we close ourselves off from receiving the full benefits of that grace. Forgiveness doesn't mean the other person was right—it means you're choosing to trust God with the situation.

☀ *The Process of Forgiveness* ☀

Forgiveness isn't always a one-time event. It's a process, and it takes faith. When negative thoughts or feelings try to creep back in, recognize them for what they are—a temptation to hold onto pain. Just because you still feel hurt doesn't mean you haven't forgiven. When you get some kind of a funny, weird feeling, or you feel animosity towards somebody, Satan comes in right away, and he says, "See there, you didn't forgive

---

Forgiveness goes beyond simply saying, "I'm sorry."
It's about real change, accepting responsibility and
understanding the power of a covenant.

---

him." A lot of people call this a lying symptom. It means you must continue standing in faith, declaring with your mouth, "I forgive them. I release them."

Supernatural forgiveness took place during the miraculous Road to Damascus weekend, but then, in walking in continued victory, a pattern of continual forgiveness is crucial. You will recall in Matthew 18:22 that Peter thought he was being very generous, asking Jesus if he should forgive his brother seven times. Jesus turned around and instructed, not seven, but seventy times seven!

Brother Hagin once shared a story about a woman struggling to forgive her mother-in-law. She insisted she hated her, but when she said it, she felt a scratchy discomfort in her heart. That was her spirit resisting the bitterness her mind was holding onto. When she started confessing love by faith, even when she didn't feel it, over time, her heart changed. The love of God was already in her, and by speaking it out, she aligned her heart with that truth.

Just because this incident was about her mother-in-law, the same goes for your husband or wife.

✺ *Boundaries and Forgiveness* ✺

It's important to note that forgiveness does not mean enabling abuse or toxic behavior. A woman with an abusive husband (Please know that this applies whether it is the husband or the wife who is the abuser) can forgive him, but that doesn't mean she must stay in harm's way. Forgiveness is a spiritual decision, but setting boundaries is a practical step. You can release resentment while also taking necessary actions to protect yourself and your family.

Each situation requires discernment. Does he need to leave until he has worked through his anger? Do you need to find a safe place? Is this a matter for the authorities? Whatever physical steps you need to take for safety, they don't negate the spiritual responsibility to forgive.

Ephesians 4:31-32 tells us to put away bitterness, wrath, and anger and instead be kind and tender-hearted, forgiving one another as Christ forgave us. That doesn't mean allowing someone to continue harming you. It means choosing not to let anger and bitterness control your heart.

One of the reasons this is so very important is found in the definition of Christ. It's not Jesus' last name. The word Christ is a Greek word. It just simply means the Anointed One and the anointing itself. Now, translate and meditate on that word, Christ. Both of them are referred to equally in that word. Let's look at it again. Even as God, **for the sake of the anointing,** has forgiven you, you can't expect faith and the anointing, the power of God, to work in unforgiveness, wrath, strife, and all of those things.

The Freedom of Forgiveness

Many people resist forgiveness because they think it lets the other person off the hook. But the truth is, it lets YOU off the hook. Holding onto bitterness is like drinking poison and expecting the other person to suffer. The Bible reminds us, "Vengeance is mine; I will repay, says the Lord." Now, don't be tempted like Brother Jesse Duplantis was one time when the Lord reminded him of that scripture. Brother Jesse told the Lord, "No! You take too long. I can fix this right now!" While we may be tempted to do that, it always works out better when the Lord handles it. When we release others into God's hands, we free ourselves to walk in joy and peace.

Forgiving Yourself

Sometimes, the hardest person to forgive is yourself. Mark 12:31 tells us to love our neighbor as ourselves.

But what if we haven't learned to love or forgive ourselves? Self-condemnation can block our faith and hinder our ability to receive God's love fully.

Forgiveness is a

daily walk.

My wife, Lynn, faced this after our reconciliation. Even after my heart softened, she battled regret— wondering if she had spoken up sooner, would things have been different? That self-condemnation was another tactic of the enemy. She had to pray, ask for God's forgiveness, and then release herself from guilt. We also discussed practical ways to ensure we handled issues differently in the future, allowing space for open and honest communication. Although these may not work for everyone, here is a list of some of the things we did.

- We started using a "couples app" that asks us questions daily, which brings up a variety of topics for us to discuss (and sometimes disagree on).

- We agreed that when Lynn is prompted to say something or has a differing opinion about something, she should bring it to my attention instead of ignoring it and not saying anything.

- We agreed that I have to be more open to opposing points of view without getting upset. This doesn't necessarily mean I must agree with everything Lynn says, but I actively listen instead of immediately dismissing it.

- We also acknowledged that mistakes could be made and emotions could flare (in other words, we wouldn't get it right every time), so we agreed to give each other some space to regroup and try again.

- Another idea is writing back and forth, which we did previously, but we chose to keep communication verbal this time to practice oral communication skills.

🔆 *Growing in Love and Grace* 🔆

Forgiveness is a daily walk. Just as God's mercies are new every morning, we must extend that same mercy—to ourselves and to others. We are all learning and growing. Every step forward is a step of faith, moving from glory to glory.

Give each other room to grow. Allow each other to make mistakes, learn, and come together with grace. The Lord will help you, just as He helped Lynn and me. I'll never forget the moment, months later, in a church service when she came to me during a time of ministry at the altar when the presence of God was very heavy. With tears in her eyes, she reassured me: "Everything is forgiven. Everything is forgiven from God; Everything is forgiven from me. We will go forward from this place—one mind, one heart, one spirit, hand in hand together."

That provided an anchor point for me. Fear had tried to sneak in on me again. The devil had begun bringing the thought to my mind, "She filed for divorce once. She will probably do it again." It was becoming a fearful thing, but you cannot afford to let fear to be working while continuing to walk in your victory. That time at the altar was a moment that solidified our decision to stand together, choosing love over fear, faith over doubt, and unity over division. And I believe He can do the same for you.

Forgiveness is never easy, but it is always worth it. Trust God, take the step, and watch as He brings healing and restoration beyond what you ever imagined.

To watch us speaking about this topic on our broadcast, scan the QR code below or type in:

https://davidweeter.org/broadcast/ forgiveness/

https://davidweeter.org/broadcast/ a-forgiving-heart/

CHAPTER

9

Living Out the Victory

☀ *Living Out the Victory* ☀

In every marriage journey, even when there has been a miraculous rebirth of the relationship, there has to be a commitment to press forward through seasons of challenge and growth and a constant pull toward unity. The Road to Damascus weekend set the stage, but we have to live out this victory. Today, let's walk through the principles that have reshaped our marriage. We'll look at how we stood in faith, built trust, and honored each other through every step.

☀ *1. Lean on God's Promises* ☀

This is no time to let go of scripture! We still remind ourselves of what the Lord did for us in accordance with Isaiah 43:19, "Behold, I will do a new thing…Now it shall spring forth…I will make a way in the wilderness and rivers in the desert." Now, it is imperative to realize where we are. At our most critical time, the Lord did the miraculous during that weekend. Now (and until Jesus returns), we have to walk out this victory. Keeping that in mind, this verse takes on a two-part nature.

Part 1: Thanksgiving is a powerful tool, and we keep ourselves in remembrance and continue to give thanks that even when it looked like there was no way forward and that our marriage was over, God was able to bring forth those new springs and rivers even in the most challenging places.

Part 2: If a spring dries up and the river quits flowing, the landscape becomes a desert once again. So we continue to press into the scripture because old habits, patterns of communication, etc., will try to come back from time to time and recreate challenges.

As we are walking this out, we especially press into 2 Thessalonians 3:16, which says, "Now may the Lord of peace Himself grant you His peace at all times and in every way." We need this peace deeply rooted in our hearts, especially when moments come, and they will come from time to time (see John 16:33) when it feels like everything around us is in turmoil. Living out the victory in marriage means standing on these promises, even when you're navigating revisited wilderness or desert moments.

2. Staying Unmoved by Circumstances

A cornerstone of faith is the ability to stand firm, regardless of current circumstances. Second Corinthians 4:18 encourages us, saying we're not moved by what we see but by the promise of what's unseen and eternal. We often face the temptation to let what we see—the challenges and frustrations—overshadow God's promises. But faith means trusting that what seems impossible now is just a stepping stone toward transformation.

In our story, we held onto the belief that if God had planned our marriage, He wasn't about to let us falter. For anyone feeling discouraged, remember: if it was God's will for you to unite as one, that doesn't change. God is still God. He never changes. If it was His will for you to marry that person, it's still His will today. Stand firm in that truth, and don't let fear or doubt rob you of the future God has planned for you.

☀ 3. Prioritize Your Partner ☀

Make your spouse feel valued. It's one thing to say they come first, but showing it through actions—both big and small—is essential. This particular point was huge for us because I had prioritized the work of the ministry (this applies to any job) over her. Obviously, this made her feel unvalued. To overcome this, I searched diligently for ways to demonstrate her level of priority in my life. For example, since work had been prioritized above her when we had conversations, I would put my phone in "do not disturb" mode, so alerts did not distract me from giving her my full attention.

Another example is that I make certain to make her coffee before I make mine. That example may seem like a small thing, but it is a continual thing, and it's a heart thing, similar to sharing a piece of cake and making sure she gets the bigger share. I also made sure to do large things. When Lynn had to be in Arkansas taking care of her father, and I would return from a ministry trip at the end of the week to Fort Worth, I would go the extra mile (actually a couple of hundred miles) by packing up the car and driving all night so that I could be there when she woke up the next morning. Now, in all honesty, part of that may have been selfishness on my part because I wanted to be with her so much.

Lynn had actually prioritized me throughout our marriage. When I would start talking, she would always do her best to stop what she was doing to give me her attention. She makes a point to make time to do things with me that I truly enjoy, like hiking, motorcycle riding, and hunting. She does her best to support any area of the ministry that is needed by jumping in and figuring out how to do whatever it is that needs to be done. She did have to make some tweaks to prioritizing our marriage by making a point to speak up when she needed something or when she saw something was straining our marriage.

4. Embracing Change by Renewing the Mind

After our pivotal transformation, we had to change the way we communicated and interacted daily. Romans 12 calls this the renewing of the mind—a process that doesn't happen overnight but requires consistent effort. A word of caution here: Satan will attempt to lay a trap in this area. When an old habit or pattern of communication shows up, he will immediately come in with the thought, "Oh, this wasn't a real change after all." I like the way Lynn put this, "the person who was offended has to press into forgiveness because old thought patterns, not heart patterns, thought patterns can still be there and have to be relearned." Old habits can be tough to overcome. It's like cleaning out a messy house, and if you let old habits slip back in, it won't be long before the mess returns. **Staying the course means guarding this renewed mindset and not becoming complacent.**

Stay Accountable: Old habits die hard. Give your spouse permission to call out old patterns when they reappear. Lynn still occasionally has to tell me, "You're doing that thing again!" The other side of that is that I have to not get upset when she does because I told her to do it and realize that it is an investment into our continued victory. This helps both of you recognize and address any lingering issues before they escalate. I also make a point of asking her if there is anything she would like to talk about to help give her an open opportunity to talk about anything on her heart or mind. This helps open up not only things that need to be addressed but also increases the overall intimacy of the relationship by discussing things like dreams, hopes, vacation ideas, etc. The opportunities are endless.

This journey of "renewing" isn't just an individual pursuit; it is a shared responsibility. We each needed to remain mindful of the new, positive habits we wanted to build while making space for one another to grow.

Seek God's Guidance: Pray together and individually. God's presence is the most vital part of any restoration process. He's able to guide you through every step. It is important to realize that God has called and anointed people to produce resources to help you with this. You're holding one of them in your hand right now! We would recommend that you re-read this book at least every six months. Even in the process of writing and editing this book, we realized that some of the principles the Lord had talked to us about had slipped a little bit. This enabled us to make adjustments, get better, and continue on our road to victory.

I would say perhaps one of the most important things you can do is to make a list of the things that have come up to you that you need to work on while you were reading this book. Once you have that list, it is time to go to 1 Corinthians 11. In this chapter, Paul explains how to take communion in verses 23-32. Let me draw your attention specifically to verses 28-32.

[28] But let a man examine himself, and so let him eat of *that* bread, and drink of *that* cup.

[29] For he that eateth and drinketh unworthily, eateth and drinketh damnation to himself, not discerning the Lord's body.

[30] For this cause, many *are* weak and sickly among you, and many sleep.

[31] For if we would judge ourselves, we should not be judged.

[32] But when we are judged, we are chastened of the Lord, that we should not be condemned with the world.

Now, take the list and do precisely what the scripture says, examine yourself, and be completely honest because if we judge ourselves, we should not be judged. Take communion and ask the Lord to help you in these areas. Set a reminder on your calendar (phone or whatever you use) to go back and look at the list again in three months (or whatever time frame God tells you), honestly examine yourself again, and see where you are. After this process, when you read the book the next time, adjust your list and repeat the process.

In addition to our books, there are many scripturally based resources for improving communication, building

Old habits can be tough to overcome.

...

Staying the course means guarding your renewed mindset and not becoming complacent.

relationships, walking more fully in love, and all the other aspects of marriage. We cautioned earlier in the book about just reading anything and everything, grasping at straws, and trying to make something happen. Now we are at a place where we can encourage you to pray about and be led peacefully in which resources the Lord would have for you specifically. That's a very important key. Not every resource will minister to every person, but the Lord knows which ones you need at which times.

5. Choosing to Trust Each Other and Forgiving Often

Proverbs 31 tells us that a spouse can fully trust their partner without fear or suspicion. There's power in trusting God's design for your marriage, even when it feels vulnerable. Of course, habits from the past might creep back in, or sometimes, an old wound might trigger a reaction that doesn't reflect where you are now. Remember, those are opportunities to exercise forgiveness, a gift we can give to each other over and over.

When Jesus tells us to forgive "not seven times, but seventy times seven," He's pointing to a continuous flow of grace, which can be tough, but it's essential. Forgiveness allows space for growth and gives each person permission to try again.

On the other side of that, practice humility: When you're wrong, own it. Apologize without expecting anything in return, and let that humility be a foundation for growth.

Personally, we were both always very independent. We weren't good at school projects because nobody did their part as well as we knew we could. So, in our marriage, we truly assigned different jobs to ourselves based on each other's strengths and weaknesses. While this is a good thing in general, on the one hand, we did trust each other with those assigned jobs. The problem came in when we really needed to ask for help but didn't trust the other one to continue seeing us as competent in our "assigned" role if we asked for it. So, in reality, we didn't see ourselves as one but two independent people in a contract. We were "independent together," to quote an old Christmas movie.

6. The Armor of Love— Not Just Tough Love

True love isn't always "tough love." The famous verses in 1 Corinthians 13 describe love as patient and kind. While there are times when a firm stance is necessary, there should also be times to show softness and grace, especially within the sanctuary of marriage. Even in relationships that might feel like a battlefield, remember that home should be a place of peace.

We daily, on purpose, find ways to express love in all the "languages." We make sure we are touching each other in both sexual and non-sexual ways. We do our best to daily complement each other on something, whether it is her telling me how amazing the coffee I make is or me telling her how absolutely stunningly beautiful she is. We try to make sure we do something for the other person daily (that typically means something that they would do for themself, we do for them), like me filling her gas tank or her setting out my daily vitamins to make sure I take them. We make sure we have quality time together every night by shutting down all of the work after we eat supper. We don't typically get gift-giving in every day, but it can really be as simple as bringing home their favorite candy from the trip to the store.

A lot of guys have a tendency to have a "tough love," military-type view of love, but let's look at Deuteronomy 10:16: "Circumcise therefore the foreskin of your heart, and be no more stiffnecked." As a man, we are acutely aware that whatever has been circumcised becomes very tender! So, gentlemen, listen to the Word and allow the Lord and your wife to help you develop a more tender heart.

In our marriage, we learned that the "armor of God" is meant for spiritual battles against unseen forces, not as a weapon against our spouse or family. There's a time for firm resolve, but there's also a need to create an environment where each person feels safe and valued. It's a delicate balance, but one that transforms a home into a place of peace.

Now, there is a time to fight! Fight those principalities and powers that are trying to attack your new marriage. Fight with everything you have (i.e., the Word and your and your spouse's agreement) to keep them from interfering by way of stealing, killing, and destroying within your marriage. Those little devils will try to sneak back in, especially in the area of old thought patterns and habits, by magnifying misunderstandings and trying to stir up strife and confusion. Don't let them do it!

✹ 7. Pressing into the Covenant with God as the Anchor ✹

Let me drop a life tip here: this isn't just about marriage; it applies to everything in life.

Sometimes you're just going about your day, doing your best, and *bam,* you get hit with something out of nowhere, like a gut punch from the enemy when you least expect it. In those moments, you've *got* to lean into your covenant with God. Cling to it. Stand on it. However you want to say it, just trust in it. God is faithful. He keeps His promises.

You probably remember from the last chapter, when I got served those divorce papers, it felt like my insides were ripped out. No exaggeration, I ended up on the floor in full-on, ugly-cry, can't-breathe sobs. And yeah, I know it sounds dramatic, but I'm being real with you. In that moment, it felt like my life was over. I was drowning in hopelessness. My mind and emotions were just spiraling…fast.

Every Scripture I thought of would instantly be countered by some thought like, "Yeah, but that doesn't apply to you because of x, y, or z." It was spiritual warfare at its finest.

If you ever find yourself in a place like that, here are two things that helped me, and I believe they'll help you too.

First, pray in tongues. Romans 8:26 tells us that when we don't know how to pray, pray in the Spirit. When we do that, the Spirit steps in and prays *through* us, and He knows exactly what needs to be said, even when we don't.

Second, press into your covenant with God. Remind yourself that your Father is a covenant-keeping God. That doesn't change, no matter what your circumstances look like.

In a covenant marriage, God is the anchor, and this covenant is powerful. There were many times when I cried out to God, reminding Him (and myself) that He's my covenant-keeping God and putting pressure on the covenant rather than on my spouse. This is a key principle: if you're tempted to manipulate or pressure your partner, shift that focus toward God. Allow Him to be the One who guides, heals, and renews both of you.

Pressing into your covenant means acknowledging that God, as the covenant keeper, can do more in a moment than any amount of coaxing or controlling ever could. Let Him carry the weight of that covenant, and trust Him with the outcome.

8. Honoring Each Other's Gifts

Every marriage combines unique strengths and gifts that God has placed within each partner. Honoring these differences means seeing them not as points of conflict but as complements. For example, my directness often needs to be tempered by Lynn's gracious approach, and

In a covenant marriage, God is the anchor, and this covenant is powerful.

it's in this blend that we find balance. However, sometimes a little bluntness is needed.

I remember one time during a family situation where I needed to step up and take charge. Our daughter even texted Lynn to say, "Let Dad off the leash." But Lynn would give me a little nudge or a touch on the hand when I was getting too intense, and I'd ease back just enough. We honored each other's gifts in that moment, knowing that God brought us together to complement each other, not to compete. And by the way, that situation was resolved perfectly.

There's beauty in this harmony, like a musical chord, with each note contributing to the overall sound. When we honor these differences, we're more equipped to face life's challenges together. The synergy we create can impact others in ways we couldn't reach on our own.

☀ *Final Thoughts: Living Out the Victory* ☀

Sharing this journey has been difficult at times but also a joy. Our story is a testament to God's ability to rebuild and renew, to take what was once broken and make it whole. No matter where you are in your marriage or how difficult things may seem, God has a plan for victory, one that doesn't just keep you together but draws you closer than ever before.

God's gift of restoration is available to us all. It requires humility, patience, and a willingness to press into true repentance. But if we remain open, God can do miraculous things in our relationships, taking us from brokenness to wholeness. He promises a fresh start— like the sunrise on a new day—and with His guidance, we can experience lasting peace and joy together.

We are now living out this victory, and as we continue, we feel empowered knowing that God is our foundation. So stand firm, trust Him, honor each other's gifts, and know that together, you are unstoppable.

To watch us speaking about this topic on our broadcast, scan the QR code below or type in:

https://davidweeter.org/broadcast/restoration/

https://davidweeter.org/broadcast/living-out-the-victory/

www.ingramcontent.com/pod-product-compliance
Lightning Source LLC
Chambersburg PA
CBHW071134280326
41935CB00010B/1229